RAF AIRCRAFT TODAY:2
LIGHTNING

RAF AIRCRAFT TODAY:2
LIGHTNING

Arthur Reed

LONDON

IAN ALLAN LTD

First published 1984

ISBN 0 7110 1407 8

Published by Ian Allan Ltd, Shepperton, Surrey;
and printed by Ian Allan Printing Ltd at their works
at Coombelands in Runnymede, England.

CONTENTS

Cover:
Lightning Mk 6 XS899 of No 5 Squadron Binbrook.
Lindsay Peacock

1
LIGHTNINGS — A QUANTUM JUMP

Below:
The P1 original prototype is prepared for one of its early flights from Boscombe Down airfield, preferred by the test pilot, Wg Cdr R. P. 'Bee' Beamont, because of its longer runway compared with the company airfield at Warton, Lancashire. First flight of the P1 was on 4 August 1954. *British Aerospace (BAe)*

When the English Electric (later BAC, now British Aerospace) Lightning fighter design was sketched on the back of the proverbial envelope in 1947, its specification represented a quantum jump forward for both the British aircraft industry and the Royal Air Force.

Only seven years earlier, soon after the start of World War 2, the RAF still had the Gloster Gladiator biplane fighter in front-line squadron service, and although the conflict against Germany had given a tremendous impulse to the march of aviation technology, the industry and the Service was still on the threshold of the jet, with the Meteor F4 (top speed 585mph) and the Vampire (540mph) the peak of contemporary technology.

So the Lightning proposal, with its 60deg wing sweepback, two jet engines mounted on top of each other inside a slab-sided fuselage, advanced avionics to turn the aircraft into a flying platform for shooting down with missiles enemy bombers, all-flying tail, powered controls, and a projected top speed of 1,500mph, was a giant leap.

Such a leap was hard to swallow by the Ministry of Supply and the Royal Aircraft Establishment, Farnborough, but swallow it they did in the shape, in 1947, of an experimental study contract, ER 103, and two years later, a contract, F23/49, for two prototypes and an airframe for static test.

To overcome RAE doubts that the sweepback proposed by English Electric was too much, the Government had a test aircraft, the SB5, specially developed by Short Brothers, of Belfast, with wings which could be swept at different angles, and a tail which could be tried high or low. All this proved was that the English Electric team had, in fact, got it right, and the opinion in the aircraft industry was that the Government of the day, in pursuing a timid 'belt-and-braces' approach had simply wasted both time and public money.

In fairness, the EE team was generally very young, and some of them had little experience in designing aircraft. The project was 'born' in a garage in the centre of Preston, Lancashire, which had been acquired a few years earlier by English Electric for the team which designed the Canberra, as classic a bomber as was the Lightning a classic fighter, but of far more conventional design. There the chief engineer of the EE aviation division, W. E. W. 'Teddy' Petter formed a key group, the leading members of which were, Ray Creasey, chief aerodynamicist, Dai Ellis, chief of flight test and wind tunnels, Harry Harrison, chief production engineer, F. W. Page, chief of stress, and Wg Cdr R. P. 'Bee' Beamont, chief test pilot, the latter remaining the project pilot with sole responsibility for the flight testing evaluation programme from 1948 until his last Lightning test flight in 1968, a remarkable record.

The P1, predecessor to the Lightning, was virtually hand-crafted at the EE works at Warton airfield, but then production of the major sections was shifted to the centre of Preston, and to Accrington. The large sections were taken by road to the EE airfield at Samlesbury, not far from Warton, where the final assembly line was established, and the first flight of each aircraft was from Samlesbury to Warton, from where (apart from first flight, and some early operations from the Government test establishment at Boscombe Down) all of the test flying took place.

The P1, powered by two Sapphires, and targeted to have a maximum speed of Mach 1.2, made its maiden flight, with Beamont at the controls, from Boscombe Down on 4 August 1954, without any problems, apart from a radio breakdown. Before then, the Air Ministry had shown such enthusiasm for the project that it had ordered the P1B, the fighter variant of the P1 with Mach 2 performance. The P1B was a very different aircraft to the P1 and the second prototype, the P1A, having Avon 24R engines with reheat, provision for a full weapons system, with Ferranti radar, and a new round nose intake section with a centre-body, inside which the radar was housed. First flight of the P1B was on 4 April 1957, which happened to be the same day that the Conservative Government of that day published its White Paper forecasting the end of manned aircraft, and their replacement by missiles.

Several other British military aircraft projects were cancelled in this traumatic period for the British aircraft industry, but the Lightning survived and remains in squadron service with the RAF at the time of writing, spring, 1983.

Above right:
Whether the aircraft which became the Lightning should have a high or low tail was a debate which exercised the minds of the designers in the late 1940s. Two of the 'backs-of-envelope' sketches are reproduced here.

Right:
WG760, the P1 prototype, was posed by English Electric for one of the first publicity shots — a very different shape to the aircraft which serves with the Royal Air Force today. *Derek Wood*

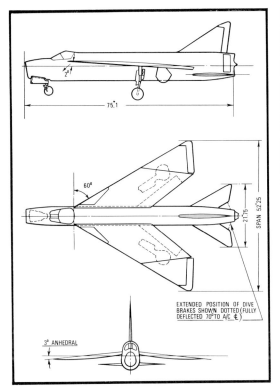

60°

75.1

21.75 SPAN 5.2.25

2°

EXTENDED POSITION OF DIVE
BRAKES SHOWN DOTTED (FULLY
DEFLECTED 70°TO A/C ¢)

3° ANHEDRAL

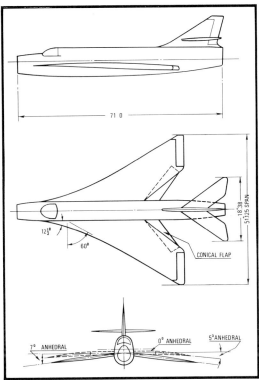

71 0

18.38 SPAN
5.1.125 SPAN

12½°

60°

CONICAL FLAP

7° ANHEDRAL   0° ANHEDRAL   5° ANHEDRAL

Left:
Bee takes a nostalgic look at the cockpit which was his air-borne 'office' during hundreds of test flights as the development programme progressed from P1 into the fully-fledged Lightning. *BAe*

Below:
Members of the English Electric ground staff put the final touches to the P1 at Warton before it is towed out for disposal at the end of its useful life. *BAe*

Right:
The P1 'grandfather' aircraft of the Lightning programme stood as a 'gate guardian' at the RAF apprentice college at Henlow from June, 1967. *BAe*

Below right:
By 1983, the P1 prototype had been transferred from Henlow to RAF Binbrook, home of the two remaining Lightning squadrons, where it was refurbished into sparkling condition. *Author*

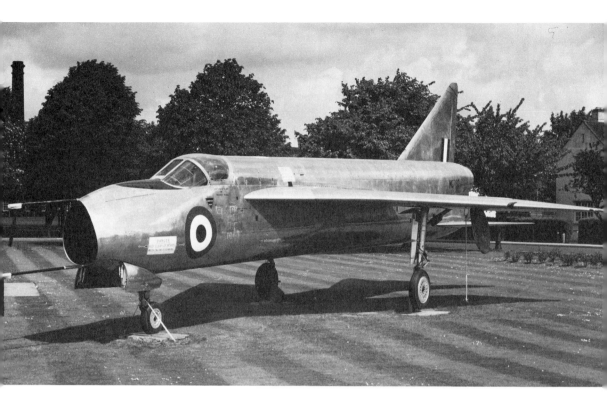

Left:
Detail of the undercarriage of the P1 WG760 restored at Binbrook, in 1983. *Author*

Below:
P1 out above the clouds on an early development sortie.
Derek Wood

Bottom:
Those testing days. With Bee 'up', the P1 banks gracefully away from the Meteor photographic aircraft. *Derek Wood*

Right:
Bee brings WG760 over the top of the camera plane, displaying the P1's advanced lines, for that era, and its distinctive fish-mouth inlet. *Derek Wood*

Below right:
A contrast in types. Bee stands by the P1 to watch the progress of the Wren, built in 1922, at Warton. *Derek Wood*

Above:
There is something very definitely aquatic about the P1A prototype as it closes in on the chase aircraft. The nose of the aircraft was radically altered later, with a round intake incorporating a 'bullet' housing the radar. *Derek Wood*

Left:
Beautiful vertical view shows the plan of the P1A prototype, WG763, powered, like the P1, by two Sapphires, rather than the Avons of later versions. *Derek Wood*

Below left:
The P1B prototype, XA847, had the rounded nose of later Lightnings, and was the first British aircraft to fly at Mach 2 — on 25 November 1958. The aircraft is now in the RAF Museum, Hendon, London. *Derek Wood*

Above right:
Staff from the English Electric hangar and technical office were assembled to pose in front of the P1, which wears its 'fencer's mask' air intake blank. In the group are (ninth from right) F. W. Page, who led the development team, and (11th from right) test pilot Beamont. *BAe*

Right:
On an appearance, probably in 1957, over its home airfield at Warton, the P1 does a tight turn around the new English Electric control tower. By that time, cambered leading edges had been fitted. *The Times*

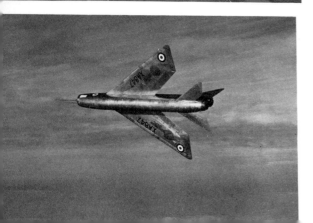

Top:
The Government ordered the SB5 from Shorts to check the English Electric calculations on the Lightning. Opinion at EE was that the project was a wasted effort. Aircraft is pictured here at Boscombe Down, in 1953. *Shorts*

Above:
Wings of the SB5 could be altered on the ground to different angles of sweep, and the tail placed at varying heights. Aircraft is seen here with 60deg sweepback, and low tailplane, in May 1954. *Shorts*

Top centre:
Similarities to the Lightning of the SB5 can be identified in this September 1960 picture, taken at RAE Bedford. Wings here are swept back 96deg. *Shorts*

Top right:
Plan view of the SB5, at Bedford, in 1960, shows the wings in the fully-swept position. *Shorts*

Right:
According to Sir Frederick Page, one good thing which came out of the SB5 project was the identification of the problem of lateral rocking at circuit speeds, solved by introducing a small 'notch' into the leading edge of the wings. Aircraft seen here is flying over Bedford in November 1960. *Shorts*

Left:
Prototype P1B XA847 was used for a time at RAE Farnborough for tests into the stopping power of beds of gravel, polystyrene balls, and other materials. The nose was blanked off to prevent engine damage, and in this picture the aircraft has an extended fin, dating from earlier trials. *RAE*

Below:
A series of scale models of the Lightning wing shape were made at Warton and Preston to test the 60deg sweepback, and were flown on rocket motors produced by the English Electric guided weapons division at speeds of up to Mach 1.85. These models were fired at the army ranges at Larkhill in 1954 to show whether such a design would be liable to flutter, as there was a dearth of theoretical information. The telemetry traces showed that although the wing did vibrate, it was damped, and there was no flutter, nor divergence. *BAe*

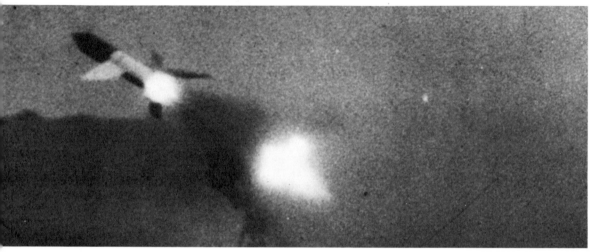

Above:
Final manufacturing touches are put to an early Lightning. Producing such a modern aircraft was a great challenge to English Electric, taxing the engineering ingenuity of everybody in the company. *BAe*

Below:
Large sections of Lightnings were built up in jigs, then joined together with other sections. Titanium was introduced, probably for the first time in British aerospace engineering, and was used in the engine bay to resist high temperatures. *BAe*

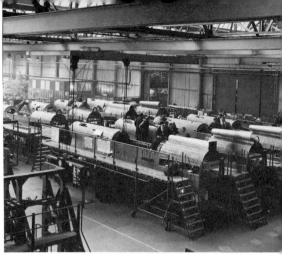

Above:
Nose sections of Lightnings on the assembly line at the English Electric Strand Road works, Preston, where railway carriages and tramcars had been produced in an earlier era. *BAe*

Above right:
Rear sections, from the tail to just behind the cockpit, in profusion. EE's Strand Road factory was tooled up to produce six Lightnings a month, but the rate never exceeded four a month during the production period, which ran from 1960 to 1968. *BAe*

Below:
Cockpit sections are already 'stuffed' with many of the systems in this view of the Lightning production line. *BAe*

Right:
Two cockpit sections ready for completion. *BAe*

Below right:
The main sections of the fuselage have been mated in this picture. Final assembly took place at Samlesbury, to where the sections were transported by road. *BAe*

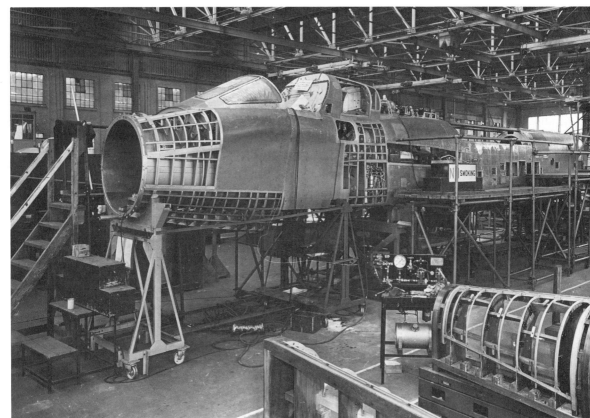

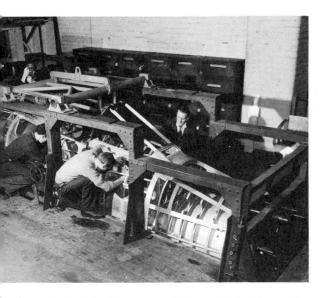

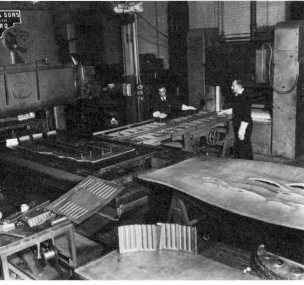

Top:
Nose section in the jig. Largely to make access easier for workers, the nose section of each Lightning was made in two sections split from front to back. *BAe*

Above:
Lightning parts emerge from EE's big press. Manufacturing techniques developed for the Lightning programme were incorporated into later aircraft from the same stable, such as the Jaguar and the Tornado. *BAe*

Right:
Later marks of Lightnings, with the square-topped, rather than the pointed tail, crowd the EE assembly shop. Welding was introduced into the primary structure to an extent which had not been used in airframe construction in Britain before. *BAe*

Right:
Rolls-Royce Avon RA24 engines superseded in the P1Bs the Armstrong Siddeley Sapphires which were fitted to the P1 and P1A. *BAe*

Centre right:
The Rolls Avon RB146 was an uprated version of the original Avons, and was fitted to some later Lightnings. *BAe*

Far right:
An early Lightning produces a spectacular plume of smoke as it runs up its Avons into an engine muffler at Boscome Down.
MoD via Mike Hooks

Below:
The dramatic still from the manufacturer publicised the two-seat T4 Lightning, with crew in full pressure suits. The trainer had, it was said, performance fully comparable to the single-seater, with the side-by-side seating accommodated within a front fuselage only $11\frac{1}{2}$ in wider.
BAe

2
CHAMPAGNE CHRISTENING

Below:
The first Lightnings for the RAF went to the Central Fighter Establishment, Coltishall, Norfolk, in December 1959, and the first operational unit, also at Coltishall, received them in July the following year. English Electric announced in March 1958 that the P1B, pictured here, had been ordered into quantity production. By that time, EE said, prototypes had completed nearly 1,000 test flights, and the P1B had exceeded 1,132mph. It could be fitted with a Napier Double-Scorpion rocket engine for very high-altitude flying — a project which was not proceeded with. *Derek Wood*

The then Chief of the Air Staff, Sir Dermot Boyle, broke a bottle of champagne to christen the Lightning in a ceremony at RAE Farnborough on 23 October 1958, and an official announcement that the type had achieved Mach 2 was made on 6 January the following year (the P1 had broken the world speed records, standing at 1,132mph, in mid-July 1957).

First flight of the T4 two-seat version of the Lightning was made in May 1959, when it was said that its performance was comparable with that of the single-seater. The development programme was not, however, devoid of problems. On a test sortie in 1959, the prototype being flown by Mr J. W. C. 'Johnny' Squier suffered a major structural failure of the tail fin, as a result of which he became the first man to bail out safely from an aircraft travelling faster than the speed of sound. Mr Squier landed in the sea and floated in his rubber dinghy for over 28 hours before coming ashore in Scotland, and as a result of the accident, the fin of the Lightning was 'beefed up', and given a different profile.

Experiments fitting the Napier Double Scorpion rocket motor to the aircraft were mooted at around this time, but were not pursued, even though the Canberra had set a new altitude record in August 1957 with such a boost. The first Lightnings went to the Central Fighter Establishment of the Royal Air Force, at RAF Coltishall, in December 1959, and the first operational unit received them in July the following year. The RAF was proud to have its new mount shown off at the Farnborough show in the autumn of 1960. Three armament combinations had been settled upon for the Service: two Firestreak air-to-air homing missiles and two 30mm cannon; two batteries of 24 2in air-to-air rockets and two 30mm cannon; or four 30mm cannon.

The first big 'stretch' of the Lightning was the Mk 3, which first flew on 16 June 1962, and which, with Avon 301(302) engines, compared with Avon 210s in the Mk 1 series, and with fully-variable reheat, had a highly-potent climb performance. As it went into RAF service in April 1964, stories abounded that it had been able to intercept in practices the United States Lockheed U-2 'spy 'plane' flying nine miles high, 'and sit effortlessly on its wingtip'.

In addition to more-powerful engines, the Mk 3 had advanced radar, navigation and fire-control equipment, a cambered leading edge, and a ventral fuel tank. The two latter changes had the effect of giving the aircraft extended patrol time, greater reheat acceleration capacity, and longer supersonic endurance. They also helped to add to the role of the Lightning as an interceptor for the defence of Great Britain that of 'fireman' for outbreaks of hostilities overseas, using its new tankage and in-flight refuelling.

The Mk 3 was later developed into the ultimate version of the Lightning, the Mk 6, which made its first flight on 17 April 1964. Basically, this was a Mk 3, but with longer range. Overwing tanks could be added for ferrying, and later models had two lower 30mm Aden guns in the longer ventral tank. By this time, the weapons had become exceptionally sophisticated for the time. The aircraft could accelerate to twice the speed of sound in $3\frac{1}{2}$ minutes, use its fire-control system to make a search of the sky, lock on to its target, approach under computer-generated steering guidance, and attack with missiles, rockets, or gunfire.

Red Top collision-course missiles were the principal interception weapon, and could be fired singly, or in pairs from above or below the target. With an eye on the export market, the Lightning was also being promoted at the time as a supersonic high or low-level reconnaissance vehicle, and as having a ground-attack capability, with two 1,000lb bombs, or launchers delivering a total of 36 SNEB 68mm rockets. Other weapons combinations offered by BAC included Matra rocket launchers carried on top of the wings, with a total of 72 SNEB rockets, and four 1,000lb bombs.

Lightnings were sold to both Saudi Arabia and Kuwait, but efforts to have it designated as NATO's main fighter failed in favour of the Lockheed F-104 Starfighter.

For the RAF introducing it into service, the Lightning represented an enormous challenge, representing as it did a 100% increase in speed and climb performance over anything that it had in its inventory. Pilots flying the first aircraft to reach the Central Fighter Establishment found that they could reach the tropopause using cold power in three to four minutes, and using reheat touch 30,000ft in two minutes. It was the first fighter which the RAF had brought into service with an all-weather capability, and CFE had to look very closely at this aspect to ensure that the workload was such that could be accepted for a single-seat operation.

As a defender of the UK, the new aircraft was expected to be able to intercept from a standing start on the ground Soviet bombers of the 'Badger, 'Bison' and 'Bear' type, after they had been picked up on radar, and before they could reach a position to launch a guided weapon. This the Lightning's predecessors, the Hunters and the Javelins, had been hard pressed to accomplish, but with its sprint performance, the new aircraft closed the gap.

One important limitation, however, was the Firestreak missile which it carried as its main armament. Firestreak was essentially a pursuit weapon, which meant that pilots had to take their Lightnings round the back of a target to ensure that the missile acquired the heat from the rear end of the enemy's jet engines. Red Top, which was prompted by this shortcoming, had a sensitivity sufficient for it to be able to home in on jet efflux from abeam, or on the kinetic heating of the skin of a supersonic aircraft.

Above:
The new fighter was officially christened in a ceremony at RAE Farnborough on 23 October 1958. In this historic picture, the Chief of the Air Staff, Sir Dermot Boyle, is shaking hands with the Chairman of English Electric, Sir George Nelson. To their right, the RAF standard which had covered the roundel and the name on the nose before the unveiling ceremony has fallen behind the dummy Firestreak missle carried by the aircraft. Hopes were expressed at the ceremony of a sale of Lightnings to the United States, but were never fulfilled. *The Times*

Top:
Twelve Mk 1s in immaculate line-up on the No 74 Squadron apron. *Derek Wood*

Above:
Very early Lightnings. The first four in this formation of Mk 1s, Nos XM135-138, were delivered to the Air Fighting Development Squadron, Coltishall, later to become the Central Fighter Establishment. The rear aircraft, XM165, was delivered to No 74 Squadron. *Derek Wood*

Top right:
Flying in formation with a Hunter Mk 6 (centre) and a Javelin Mk 5 (rear), this Lightning Mk 1 is one of a pre-production development batch of three which was delivered to the Air Fighting Development Squadron, at Coltishall, whose badge it wears on the fin. Picture was taken in 1960. *MoD*

Below:
No 74 Squadron Mk 1, armed with Firestreak, sets up a shock wave as it makes a low-level pass. *BAe*

Bottom:
The noise from the camera position must have been shattering as one of the first No 74 Squadron aircraft, XM145, runs up its Avons in reheat. *BAe*

Far left:
Two views of No 74 Squadron in very close formation. Each aircraft is armed with Firestreaks. The formation is led in each picture by XM147, which was the final aircraft in the first batch (139-147) to go to No 74. *BAe*

Above:
Lightning XM147 is in the lead again in this superb air-to-air as No 74 Squadron shows off its new mounts. *BAe*

Left:
XM214, a Mk 1A, leaves a ghostly shock wave. Aircraft was serving with No 111 Squadron. *MoD*

Below:
The distinctive Lightning flash through the RAF roundel was a 'natural' for a fighter so-named, and was claimed early by No 56 Squadron, at Wattisham. Aircraft are Mk 1As.
Derek Wood

Above left:
Mk 1A XM171, one of an early batch delivered to RAF Wattisham, poses over a sunlit cloudscape. *BAe*

Left:
No 56 Squadron Mk 1A Lightnings had a highly-distinctive colour scheme, the natural silver of the aluminium airframe being tricked out with bright red on the fuselage top, fin, and leading edges of wings and tail. A red and white chequer went through the roundel, red, white and blue colours were carried on the fin leading edge, and the squadron phoenix badge had the bird in yellow rising from a red fire on a white circle background. *BAe*

Above:
No 111 Squadron Lightnings visit RAF Akrotiri, Cyprus, during 1974, carrying Red Top missiles. Aircraft in the background appear to be of No 56 Squadron. *MoD*

Right:
No 19 Squadron lines up its Lightnings on the apron at RAF Leconfield on 23 September 1965 before moving to Gütersloh, Germany, where it became fully operational as part of the NATO front line early the following year. *The Times*

Above:
An impressive row of No 74 Squadron's Mk 1As. Careful counting totals 11 aircraft in the line-up. *BAe*

Below:
Reflections on a rainy apron of the Mk 3s for which No 74 Squadron exchanged their original Mk 1s. *BAe*

Top:
This early-model Lightning is only feet off the tarmac on take-off, but the main wheels are already tucked away, and the undercarriage doors are beginning to close. *BAe*

Above:
This was the precursor of the ultimate Lightning, the Mk 6 prototype, on test here with a backdrop of the Blackpool tower and seafront from Warton airfield with Wg Cdr Beamont at the controls. Distinguishing features are a large ventral pack beneath the aircraft belly, twin stabilising fins at the rear, and the square-topped tail, 'beefed up' after an earlier fin failure. *BAe*

Top left:
No 29 Squadron Lightnings prepare to return to their home base at RAF Wattisham from Akrotiri, Cyprus, in 1974. The squadron exchanged its Lightnings for Phantoms at the end of that year. *Ian Allan Library (IAL)*

Left:
This was the end of an epic journey for the Mk 3s of No 74 Squadron. They had just flown the 8,500 miles from their base

in Scotland to RAF Tengah, Singapore, having been refuelled in flight by Victor 2 tankers, to take over an air defence role as part of Britain's Far East Air Force. *Derek Wood*

Above:
Air brakes extended, a Mk 3 of No 111 Squadron stands on the Akrotiri flight line in January 1974. *IAL*

Above:
Two air-to-air views of XP697 fitted with twin 260gal overwing fuel tanks and a flight-refuelling probe. Overwing tanks are still on the inventories of the remaining Lightning squadrons today, but are little used. Most Lightning pilots dislike carrying them, as although they do generate a small extra amount of lift, they also produce drag, and raise fuel consumption. *BAe*

Left:
Mk 6 Lightnings of No 23 Squadron from RAF Leuchars, Scotland, in a formation remarkable for its 'togetherness'. *MoD*

Below:
The Lightning may be a big, powerful aeroplane, but it can also be extremely graceful, as this picture of No 23 Squadron Mk 6s above a sea of clouds proves. *MoD*

Above right:
The maple leaf on the fins identify these Mk 6s flying across the UK coastline as No 5 Squadron aircraft. *MoD*

Right:
The phenomenal power off the ground in re-heat of the Lightning is graphically illustrated. Once again, the main wheels are up only a few feet off the runway, with the nosewheel yet to cycle. *IAL*

Left:
Mk 6s of No 5 Squadron in line abreast. *MoD*

Below:
The massive ventral tank and twin stabilising fins of the Mk 6 are shown to good effect in this shot of a No 11 Squadron formation. The aircraft carry Red Top missiles. *MoD*

Right:
Doing the job it was designed to do. A Mk 6 of No 23 Squadron, armed with Red Tops, shepherds a Soviet 'Bear' long-range reconnaissance aircraft as it nears British airspace. Picture was taken in 1975 when No 23 was operating out of Leuchars. The squadron converted to Phantoms later that year. *MoD*

Below right:
Four No 11 Squadron Mk 6s formate against the background of the Forth rail and road bridges. *MoD via P. Collins*

Above:
Mk 6 of No 23 Squadron, with Firestreaks, flies through
sunshine and cloud. Aircraft is in original metal, apart from
roundels and red, white and blue flash, squadron crest, and bar
through roundel on nose.   *BAe*

Below:
Mk 2A Lightnings of No 19 Squadron stand on the flight line
at the British Aircraft Corporation works.   *BAe*

Above right:
Silhouetted against the sky, five Lightnings show their arrow-
head design shape as they hurry off on an exercise, their
Avons leaving faint trails in their wake.   *BAe*

Right:
How close can you get? These two pictures of the same
formation of Mk 6s prove with what precision the aircraft can
be flown.   *Image in Industry*

3
A NEW SCIENCE

Above:
An F2A reworked from the F2, and with all the appearances of
a Mk 6, stands ready to scramble in a quick-reaction hangar
with No 19 Squadron at RAF Gütersloh, Germany. *MoD*

Lightning pilots had to learn a new science — the interpretation of radar and the problems of mental trigonometry, and a new instructor category, the IWI, or interceptor weapons instructor, was evolved by the RAF to exploit the Lightning in its all-weather interceptor role.

Air Cdre Peter Collins, who was a member of the CFE team which introduced the Lightning into RAF service in 1959, and who was Officer Commanding RAF Gütersloh, West Germany, in 1976, when the type was phased out of RAF service abroad, described the Lightning as, 'Always a pilot's aeroplane, and very responsive to fly — I have rarely flown an aircraft which gave more pilot satisfaction.

'It is a very good turning aircraft, which means it can be used very effectively in the traditional air combat manoeuvres, and it had very high potential in the vertical plane. As the tactical situation developed, we realised that the development of the Lightning from its original concept into a pure missile-carrier, which it had become with the Mk 3 version, was a road which perhaps we should not have taken — that perhaps we should have kept the guns, and one of the major later developments was to restore the guns. In a close air combat situation you need guns, and you are at a disadvantage if your only weapons have a minimum range of release of something approaching a mile.

'On the central front in Germany, the Lighting became almost totally divorced from its original concept, for it was rarely able to act as a radar-equipped interceptor, or to use its high rate of climb or supersonic performance to any extent. It was more often required to provide defence against low-flying targets, engaging them, almost certainly with its guns, in visual conditions. It is entirely to the credit of the aircraft that it was able to cope very successfully with this new task, and to continue to do so right up to the beginning of 1977, when it was withdrawn from service on the central front. It took part in mock combat with a whole range of aircraft of a later generation, including Phantoms, Harriers, F-104s, and G91s, and showed up very well.'

Air Cdre Collins said that the Lightning's main problems in operations at low altitude was its high fuel consumption. 'Its turning performance has always been pretty good, and although it is not an ideal aircraft to see out of, the tactics devised for it in the central region were excellent, so that pilots soon became highly-skilled at seeing their targets in time to reach an attack position. Its very rapid acceleration made it very difficult to avoid in an intercept situation.'

After withdrawal from the central region of Germany, there were two Lightning squadrons left in the UK, and their role was to meet the threat to the UK, seen principally as low-level attacks by aircraft such as Backfire and Fencer. But they still retained an ability to intercept high-level intruders. Up against

'Backfire', the Air Commodore said, the Lightning could still be expected to give a good account of itself, for although the aircraft was highly supersonic, it would not be expected to be supersonic at low level, except in the final stages of an attack. It would therefore be important to detect it early enough.

'The Lightning has now become part of a highly-integrated defence team, of which the major elements are the ground radar system, airborne early warning, and the tanker force. There is no doubt that once the modern threat is detected, the Lightning's aerodynamic performance remains entirely adequate to take care of reaching a weapons-launching position. It is still as fast as a Phantom, and it accelerates quicker than a Phantom. Its limitation is in its weapon system, and in the number and type of weapons that it carries.' (Studies for the Lightning to carry Sidewinder missiles were in being in early 1983.)

Efforts to sell the Lightning in the world export market never achieved break-through proportions, in spite of success in the Middle East, largely because successive British governments failed to grasp the opportunity to order the development of the aircraft to its full potential, particularly in the areas of enhanced range and weapons fits.

Above left:
Phantoms began to take over from Lightnings during the 1970s both in Britain and Germany. Here the two types fly alongside each other during a formal handing-over ceremony. *MoD*

Left:
During battle exercises at RAF Gütersloh, No 19 Squadron

groundcrew wear 'hostilities kit', for protection against contamination, while rearming a Lightning. *MoD*

Above:
Mk 2A of No 19 Squadron flies past the Herman's Denkmal monument during a special flight on 4 August 1975, the 25th anniversary of the first flight. Aircraft was flown by Air Cdre Peter Collins, commanding officer of RAF Gütersloh. *MoD*

Above:
Wearing the dark green camouflage adopted by squadrons in NATO, Mk 2A XN790, of No 19 Squadron, banks across a back-drop of West German countryside. *MoD*

Below:
During a Battle of Britain display in the late 1970s, Lightnings of No 23 Squadron lead Phantoms from No 43 Squadron in a formation out of RAF Leuchars, Scotland. *IAL*

Bottom left:
One of the later Mk 6s, XS903, taxies at Luqa, Malta, at the start of an exercise in October 1967. The pilot is Wg Cdr Winshid, commanding officer of No 5 Squadron. *IAL*

Bottom right:
Her active Service life over, T5 XM967, the prototype of this version of the two-seater, rests in the museum at RAF Colerne in February 1975. *IAL*

Top:
No 23 Squadron Mk 6 XR754 (which was the first Mk 6 interim standard aircraft to go to No 5 Squadron at Binbrook) taxies past a line of No 892 Squadron Phantoms during Battle of Britain Day at RAF Leuchars in September 1975. *IAL*

Above:
XM991, a T Mk 4 two-seat, was originally delivered to RAF Middleton St George. It is serving here with No 19 Squadron in NATO. *IAL*

4
NATO COMPETITION

The greatest chance came in the late 1950s when several of the NATO countries were looking for their first supersonic fighters, and the Lightning came into head-on marketing conflict with the Lockheed F-104 Starfighter, from the United States. According to Roland Beamont, the Americans, having laid down large procurements of the 104 in advance of flight testing for the USAF, then discovered very considerable operating limitations in the aircraft, and cancelled all but a few hundred of their own build, leaving a production situation ripe for offering the world, 'which they did with all their power of American salesmanship'. In this period, there was a competition going on in Bonn. West Germany was seen as the key in the European competition for a fighter. Their purchase would be followed by other NATO air forces, in the interests of standardisation and convenience.

'We believed that the Lightning had the capability to take a strong part in this competition, and we believed it even more when we learned that the main aircraft in the competition was the F-104, because although we knew this was a capable machine for getting to Mach 2, we also knew that it had very severe operational limitations. One of the reasons was because I had been over to America and flown it. We sent a high-powered team to Bonn, but it became apparent after a period that we weren't talking at the right government level. We couldn't understand why we weren't getting to the right government ministers.

'Then it was revealed, in the course of time, that we weren't getting there because HMG had let it be known in Bonn that they were not recommending further discussion with English Electric on the Lightning, as it was not considered suitable to the German requirement. At that time there was an aeroplane called the Saunders Roe rocket fighter, which was a Ministry procurement which went sour. The Saunders Roe factory was set up to build this aeroplane for the RAF, but the RAF did not want it, on technical grounds. A strong Government effort developed to sell it to Germany, in order to maintain employment in the Isle of Wight. This was a technical non-starter in the biggest possible way, for anybody who knew about it. There was no doubt at all that HMG defeated any chances of getting the Lightning into that competition, but we would have only got into that competition with a chance if we had been able to develop the fuel system at that time.

'I believe that a massive opportunity to sell Lightnings all over Europe was lost at that time, and that we could have sold half to three-quarters of the total F-104 buy. The F-104 was bought primarily for ground attack in Germany and Italy, but in a number of the smaller air forces, it was equally purchased for self-defence. The self-defence capability could have been performed by the Lightning very well indeed, and very much better than the F-104. It is likely that had the Lightning been on offer at that time, as many as 500-600 sales would have gone to it.

'The later buy of Phantoms for the RAF was logical when the Lightning was not developed subsequently further as an advanced-weapons system. The Phantom had a second-generation weapons system, with a look-down radar capability, and advanced missiles. The Lightning system was never developed after Red Top, so that it had a simple look-up system. The Phantom look-down system was very much more effective, which isn't necessarily to say that we should have gone for a Phantom purchase without considering the development of a British radar with look-down capability. With the sort of expenditure which went into the Phantom programme, the Lightning could have well been developed further. The Mk 6 Lightnings are able to go out 300-400 miles from base, and then hook up on tankers, and this is about the same radius on long-range patrol as the Phantoms have.'

Wg Cdr Beamont recalled: 'In the early 1960s, those responsible for engineering in the Service undoubtedly said to their lords and masters, this aeroplane is no good, we will never make its systems engineering right. That was said because of a considerable under-estimation of the support task necessary to keep a supersonic aeroplane flying. Once they learned how many man-hours of maintenance you have to put into a flying hour on a supersonic aeroplane, it all started to come right. Now, if you ask in the RAF at any level about Lightning serviceability, they will say, 'Old hat, it's marvellous, easy aeroplane, it'll do 45 hours per month per aeroplane, any time you like'. It was the first of its class, and it was underestimated. But it was that attitude, as much as any other factor, which prevented it from being funded up for further development, when some engineers lost faith in the Lightning in the early 1960s.'

The sale of Lightnings to Saudi Arabia and to Kuwait was clinched in 1966, but only at the end of a bitter sales competition against Lockheed, with the F-104, Northrop, with the Tiger, and Dassault, with the Mirage. Saudi Arabia took 35 Lightning Mk 53s (basically the RAF Mk 6) and seven two-seat Mk 55s (basically the T5), and Kuwait 12 Mk 53s and two Mk 55s. Additions and replacements brought the total Middle East buy up to 61. The initial purchase was worth £89million, and in the case of Saudi Arabia, the sale was the cornerstone on which the massive BAC, and now British Aerospace, support operation for the Royal Saudi Air Force was based.

The Saudis appreciated the difficulties inherent in a non-industrialised country such as theirs servicing a complex supersonic aircraft such as the Lightning, and a memorandum of understanding was signed in May 1973 with BAC under which the latter operated and developed the RSAF training structure for both air and ground crews, maintenance and support of both Lightning and Strikemaster aircraft, the development and operation of an efficient procurement and supply system, and the construction and maintenance of buildings and plant. By 1977, there were 2,000 British Aerospace employees in Saudi Arabia, with 250 workers manning the Saudi defence contract headquarters, at Warton, and more than 200 other BAe personnel providing back-up. Looking after the 'tail' of the BAe battalions was a massive task in itself. The welfare department attended not only to the needs of the 2,000 in Saudi Arabia, but those of their 10,000 or so dependents in the UK.

Below:
Mixed bag; XM971 T4 two-seater (foreground) keeps company with three Mk 3s; all carry Firestreaks. *MoD*

Bottom:
One of the earliest Mk 3s, XP694, Firestreaks at the ready, displays a perfect plan view. *BAe*

Left:
No 5 Squadron Mk 6 comes in for a landing at Luqa, Malta.
Aircraft is XS923. *IAL*

Below:
Two Mk 6s scramble in unison off the runway at RAF Akrotiri,
Cyprus. *RAF*

Bottom:
Powerful close-up as T4 two-seat taxies out. Aircraft is from
No 56 Squadron, and has the phoenix crest on the fin.
Rolls-Royce

Above:
Familiar lightning flash distinguishes this Firestreak-carrying Mk 3 as a No 111 Squadron aircraft. *MoD*

Below:
No 56 Squadron Mk 6 about to put down. In the foreground, a Canberra and, behind it, a Vulcan. *Rolls-Royce*

Above:
Lightnings frequently exercised out of Malta from their UK bases in their heyday with the RAF. Here, a No 111 Squadron Mk 3, normally based at Wattisham, banks over a Mediterranean coastline. *IAL*

Left:
Twin Matra rocket launchers carrying a total of 36 missiles under each wing were proposed for the Royal Saudi Air Force Lightnings, but the RSAF specified one such launcher under each side. Even so, with this armament, backed up by 2in rockets and the forward weapons bay, the Mk 53 was a formidable ground-attack machine. *BAe*

Below:
Close-up of a RSAF Mk 53 carrying bombs and twin retractable launchers with 44 2in rockets, fitted instead of Red Top or Firestreak. The rockets are spin-stablised, and are designed to fire with optimum dispersion for hitting the target. Two are fired in ripple salvoes every 25 milliseconds, either first from one, and then from the other launcher, or from both at the same time. The launchers themselves automatically extend outwards and downwards in one second for firing, and close again after attack. *BAe*

Above:
Red Top missile is stowed just above the port of one of the Lightning's Aden cannon, housed in the forward portion of the ventral bulge. Picture also emphasises the extreme slimness of the aircraft's high-pressure mainwheel tyres, made so to fit snugly into the thin wing. *BAe*

Below:
Impressive array of weaponry laid out before this Mk 53 standard Lightning includes Red Top and Firestreak missiles, Aden cannon and ammunition, 1,000lb bombs, and wing-mounted and weapons-bay rockets. Lightning can also carry a five-camera VINTEN reconnaissance pack as part of its ventral bulge. *BAe*

5
SALES TO THE MIDDLE EAST

Below:
Royal Saudi Air Force officers pore over the cockpit of the demonstration Lightning when the sale was being made, while VIPs are given a walk round the aircraft. The aircraft was demonstrated by Jimmy Dell, who showed off its sonic boom-making qualities, by request. *Trevor Tarr*

There is little doubt that the Saudis bought the Lightning because of its enhanced endurance and its performance as a ground-attacker following the development of the Mk 6 version. To tide the RSAF over until new-build aircraft began to arrive, they were sent interim types, Mk 2s recoded Mk 52, and Mk 4 trainers, recoded Mk 54. Lightnings for the RSAF were delivered under a programme named Magic Carpet, later Magic Palm, in which BAC test pilots made nonstop flights from the base at Warton to the Middle East, refuelling from RAF tankers on the way. Much British prestige was involved in the successful completion of these long-distance and arduous trips, and a great deal of logistical planning went into their preparation. An HS125 jet stood by with spares and a groundcrew, ready to fly to any airfield on route to which a delivery aircraft might divert, and the plan was to stage through Akrotiri, Cyprus, where the RAF had, at that time, a Lightning base. The final 'Magic Palm' flight was on 4 September 1972, piloted by Pete Ginger.

The story of the Lightning in RSAF service has been a successful one, the aircraft having formed the backbone of that country's air-defence force since 1966, when the F2s and F4s were sent out to fill the gap before delivery of the custom-built aircraft, and they will probably continue in service until the middle 1980s, when they will be superseded by the fleet of McDonnell Douglas F-15 Eagles which the Saudis were operating. The Kuwaiti story is a less-happy one. After operating their aircraft successfully for seven years, that country was then persuaded to buy French Mirages. The Lightning fleet was grounded, with inevitable deterioration in their condition in the fierce heat and sand conditions of the desert environment. Today, the official word is that they are 'in store'.

It was while in service with the Saudi air force that Lightnings fired their first and, at the time of writing, their only shots in anger. A column of rebels moved against Saudi Arabia from the south. They were halted by other aircraft from the RSAF, and the Lightnings were then sent to 'soften up' the column as it turned round. So effective were the attacks, using 2in rockets, that during the following night the leaders of the invading force sued for peace. The whole operation was adjudged an immense success, and proved that the Lightning would be a potent and highly-effective weapon in a real war.

The Saudi operation was slightly marred by one incident, but even that had a happy ending. Returning from one of the strikes, one of the Saudi pilots was forced down, ejecting over the vast and inhospitable desert which forms a major part of that country. Before leaving the aircraft, he managed to make a Mayday signal back to base, and was told to remain near his parachute, as help was on its way. This he sensibly did, while a big rescue operation was mounted. A C-130 Hercules was rapidly put in the air, crammed with medics and troops and, escorted by Lightnings, flew to the crash area. The downed pilot was spotted. While the Lightnings circled overhead, the Herk put down in the desert, the pilot was picked up, and the return was safely made to base.

Left:
British Aircraft Corporation won orders in 1966 for 37 Mk 53s and seven Mk 55s from Saudi Arabia, and for 12 Mk 53s and two Mk 55s from Kuwait, an order which with additions and replacements rose to 61 aircraft. The sale was the cornerstone for a massive and long-standing support contract with the Saudis for BAC, and now British Aerospace. The aircraft were delivered by BAC pilots under a programme code-named 'Magic Carpet', and latterly 'Magic Palm', and in this picture pilot Pete Ginger is climbing aboard for the final flight in this programme. *BAe*

Top right:
Three of a (not dissimilar) kind; from front to rear, a Mk 55 two-seat for the Kuwait Air Force, with Firestreak, a Mk 6 for the RAF, with Red Top, and a Mk 53, for the RSAF, although unpainted, with guns, 2in rockets and 1,000lb bombs. *BAe*

Above right:
A Kuwaiti Mk 53 on show at the Paris air *salon* by the British Aircraft Corporation carries an overwing Matra rocket launcher, a configuration which was not used. Aircraft wears the BAC Union Jack arrowhead flash on its nose and a British civil registration. *MoD via M. Hooks*

Right:
Three Lightnings for Saudi Arabia (foreground) and three for Kuwait (rear) stand on the flight line at BAC's airfield at Warton, Lancs, awaiting delivery. *IAL*

Above left:
Five Mk 2s and two T4s were taken off the RAF inventory to act as advance aircraft for the Saudi Arabia order while the Mk 53s and 55s, equivalent to Mk 6s and Mk 5s were being produced. Two of this early batch, the T4s, coded RSAF 54-650 and 54-651, are pictured here over the Lancashire coast before delivery, which was in August 1966. *BAe*

Left:
54-651, one of the two RAF T4s supplied to the RSAF at the beginning of the Saudi order, hooks up to a Victor tanker. *BAe*

Below left:
The Mk 53 for the RSAF, with Wg Cdr Beamont at the

controls, first flew on 1 November 1966. Here two of the batch bank over the coastline of their desert homeland. They are 53-689, and 53-693 (right). *BAe*

Above:
First flight of a two-seat Mk 55 for the Kuwait Air Force, aircraft 55-410, pictured here, was at Warton on 24 May 1968. *BAe*

Below:
This Lightning wears Royal Saudi Air Force markings, but carries the RAF Mk 6 registration XR770. *Rolls-Royce*

Left:
Two RSAF Mk 53s, air brakes extended, come in for a landing at home base in Saudi Arabia. *BAe*

Below left:
Later in their service, the RSAF Lightnings dispensed with the codings with which they left Warton and adopted new figure codings — 211 and 207 are seen in this picture. Royal Saudi Air Force appeared in large letters along the side of the fuselage. *BAe*

Right:
RSAF Mk 53 No 213 displays its ground-attack role. It carries rocket launchers on pylons beneath the wings, and has the doors of its 2in rocket bays deployed. *BAe*

Below:
Royal Saudi Air Force Mk 53 No 215 frozen at the moment of releasing practice bombs during a ground-attack exercise. *BAe*

Bottom:
Flame lights up the underbelly of this aircraft as it carries out firing trials of 2in rockets from its retractable weapons bay. *BAe*

6
QUICK REACTION ALERT

Below:
A No 5 Squadron Mk 6 hurries off the runway at its base at
RAF Binbrook, Lincolnshire, on a misty day in January 1978.
MoD

In a nondescript building near the end of the runway at the Royal Air Force station at Binbrook, in the rolling Lincolnshire countryside, lies what might be termed the 'sharp end' of Britain's air defences. The building is the quick reaction alert (QRA) centre, one of a number of RAF bases up and down the country from which is mounted the short-order response by the Service to any threat to the integrity of the nation's airspace.

In RAF terminology, it is known as the Q shed, and at Binbrook two Lightnings, their pilots, and their groundcrews are on constant, 24-hour call, ready to put aircraft into the air within the 10-minute call-out time which the RAF demands.

Binbrook is the base for the two remaining Lightning squadrons in RAF service, Nos 5 and 11, plus a training flight (a third active squadron, announced in the House of Commons in late July, 1979 a few days before the 25th anniversary of the first flight of the Lightning, to help fill the gap in the air defence of Great Britain until the Tornado filled this role, began to form, but was then cancelled in a later defence cut). The squadrons' time from being alerted to leaving the runway can be as little as six minutes.

The Q shed was occupied by No 11 Squadron when I visited the airfield, and a typical series of events leading up to a 'scramble' was demonstrated. Each pilot on Q duty spends 24 hours on call. Q1, the first man to go, remains in the Q shed, while Q2 remains nearby on the airfield, suited up, and able to reach the Q shed within a few minutes. The quick reaction alert complex has a lounge and a bedroom for the aircrew, similar facilities for groundcrew, plus a kitchen, where one of the airmen acts as cook. The hangars for the Q Lightnings adjoin these facilities, and the aircraft wait in them ready fuelled and armed, and with as many as possible of the systems warmed up without the engines actually being started. Red Top, rather than Firestreak, missiles are always carried by the Q aircraft, which are always Mk 6s, rather than 3s.

To pass the hours between alerts, the crews read or watch television, but pilots say it is difficult to settle down to any activity requiring more than a superficial level of concentration against the knowledge that the alarm could go at any minute. At night, they are allowed to sleep, but sleep can be fitful for the same reason. Calls-out at 4.30am are not unknown.

Ruling life in the Q shed is a wall-mounted loudspeaker connected directly to an operational centre at which a constant radar watch, 24 hours each day, 365 days each year, is kept on air traffic over the east coast of Britain. The speaker emits a bleep every 30 seconds to prove that it is live.

A call to action is equally likely in the middle of the day or the middle of the night. When it comes, the duty pilots press a button which alerts the groundcrew, and run for their machines. Strapped in,

they talk to the controller, who tells them what the Q call is about. It could be a practice interception of another RAF aircraft acting as 'enemy', it could be an investigation of what turns out to be an airliner, or a light aircraft whose crew have overlooked filing a flight plan, it could be a directive to fly to a missile range in Wales to fire a live missile at a Jindivik drone, or it could just be orders to 'shadow and shepherd' a Soviet reconnaissance aircraft. For obvious reasons, calls are spasmodic, and follow no set pattern. Some pilots have had three in as many days. Others have gone through a three-year tour of duty, and have had their only alert on the final day of their tour.

The majority of the 'juicy' targets formed by the Russian aircraft, the 'Badgers', 'Bears' and 'Bisons', to give them their NATO code names, go to the Phantoms based in Scotland, rather than to the more-southerly Lightnings, as the Russians are generally bound for the northern waters, or for the Atlantic. But aided by in-flight refuelling, some of the Binbrook pilots have experienced such intercepts. Almost all of the Soviet aircraft fly quite legally in international airspace, but if they do stray into UK airspace, the Lightnings have orders to escort them out again, having formed an opinion as to the intention of the incursion — is he lost, is he probing, is he going to attack, or is he perhaps defecting? The accepted code of air-to-air signals, as laid down by the United Nations aviation body, the International Civil Aviation Organisation, is used to indicate to the intruder that it is time that he, 'left the premises'.

The general RAF practice when they find a Russian is to take up station on the port side of the other aircraft so that they can be seen by its captain. Apolitical waves are often exchanged between the airmen on either side, while Russian crew members have been known to appear at the observation windows showing vacuum flasks with the implied invitation, 'Would you like a drink?'

A more serious activity on both sides is the taking of photographs with hand-held cameras, and as one Lightning pilot commented, 'It often seems like a competition up there to see who can produce the biggest Nikkomat.' What happens to the result of these high-altitude picture-taking sessions when they are returned to base the RAF will not say, but the author speculates that it is unlikely that they are all destined for the squadrons' scrap books, but rather are analysed by the intelligence branch for any signs of significant changes in the specification of the Soviet aircraft, and the equipment which they carry.

But although both sides are generally friendly when they meet up many miles high over the North Sea, just occasionally a Soviet aircraft banks gently towards its escorting Lightning as a test of RAF alertness and airmanship, while at least one Lightning pilot, concentrating on the tricky business of an intercept on a dark night, had his vision temporarily blinded when the Russians shone their equivalent of an Aldis lamp across the intervening gap between the two aircraft, and right in the cockpit.

Above:
Mk 6s from No 11 Squadron (foreground) and No 5 Squadron (rear) in close formation. *MoD*

Below:
One of the Lightnings' tasks today is to watch over Britain's booming North Sea oil and natural gas exploration industry. Here a No 5 Squadron Mk 6 banks over a rig. *MoD*

Above:
In March 1976 this Mk 3 of No 5 Squadron was paraded at RAF Binbrook to show off its new brown and green camouflage. Behind it is a Mk 5 two-seater in the earlier all-metal strip. *MoD*

Below:
Mk 3 on the Binbrook flight line in new camouflage early in 1976. *MoD*

Top:
Canopy up, a Mk 3 of No 11 Squadron is refuelled at
Binbrook *MoD*

Above:
Change of paint; No 5 Squadron aircraft lined up at Binbrook

in early 1976 alternate between new camouflage and old bare
aluminium finish. Maple leaf crest had to be highlighted
against the dark paint. Aircraft nearest camera, XS923, is a
Mk 6. *MoD*

Top:
No 5 Squadron's Mk 5 two-seater comes in for a landing.   *IAL*

Above:
Still looking a very neat and potent fighter, even though the *marque* began as a design 30 years previously. No 11 Squadron (nearest the camera) and No 5 Squadron aircraft (background) at RAF Leuchars, Scotland, in 1978. Three aircraft in the foreground are Mk 6s, Nos XR769, XR727 and XR773.   *MoD*

Above:
August 1977, and groundcrew refuel and service a No 11 Squadron Mk 3 at Binbrook. Mechanic on right of picture holds the intake blank.   *MoD*

Left:
May 1983 and a member of the Binbrook ground staff helps a No 5 Squadron pilot settle in his 'office'. In the foreground, a close-up of the nozzle of the aircraft's in-flight refuelling probe.   *Author*

Below left:
Getting down to it; RAF Binbrook mechanic peers closely into the cockpit of a Mk 6 as servicing goes on. Ground staff wear ear muffs as protection against the fiendish crack and roar of the Lightning start-up.   *Author*

Below:
Flt Lt Paul Field checks the cockpit of a No 11 Squadron Lightning in the quick-reaction alert shed at RAF Binbrook. Aircraft is one of two Mk 6s always at instant readiness.
Author

Above right:
Two No 11 Squadron Mk 6s line up on the Binbrook runway ready for take-off. In the background, a group of the station's 'decoys' — Lightnings which have ended their useful service life, but which are occasionally 'cannibalised' for parts, and which increase the numbers for the benefit of air-to-ground photographs.   *Author*

Right:
Carrying Red Top, a No 11 Squadron Mk 6 makes for the Binbrook take-off point during a busy morning of circuits and bumps.   *Author*

Above:
In the spring of 1983, Lightnings were changing over from grey and green camouflage, worn since 1976, to an all-grey finish. This Mk 6 has already had the treatment. The changeover produced controversy among Lightning pilots, who considered the grey scheme made their aircraft more visible over the sea than the grey-green finish. The new scheme was originally two shades of grey, but was amended to one. *Author*

Below:
Bravo Foxtrot, No 11 Squadron Mk 6, wears the 1976 grey-green paint job. *Author*

Above:
No 5 Squadron Mk 6 comes in over the Binbrook threshold. Runway has an arrestor device, which lies flat on the runway when not in use. Mk 6s are fitted with an arrestor hook. Tail parachutes are invariably used on landing, largely to save wear on brakes and tyres. *Author*

Below:
Binbrook's quick-reaction alert hangar — the Q shed — opens its doors. Only Mk 6 Lightnings, armed with Red Top, rather than Firestreak, do Q duty. *Author*

7
SHADOW AND SHEPHERD

Below:
A pair of Mk 6s about to make simultaneous contact with the
hoses of a Victor.   *Rolls-Royce*

With aid of in-flight refuelling from tankers, Lightnings have shadowed and shepherded Soviet aircraft for five or six hours in a single sortie, and there is no reason why they should not stay on station, with the aid of regular 'drinks', for up to nine hours at a time, by which time oil and oxygen are getting low. Pilots said that they do not become bored or tired on such lengthy outings, as is frequently the case with airline pilots flying long sectors. This is because there is always plenty to do to keep a single-seat fighter pilot busy. Once or twice, life has been made better still by the potential adversary. Lightning pilots tell the story of how, during a shepherding operation, one of their number, running low on fuel, called up his attendant tanker on the radio and said, 'I'll have to come in for some more gas soon. Where are you?' A voice with the thickest of Russian accents then broke in on the wavelength to give the exact latitude and longitude of the RAF tanker aircraft.

Nos 5 and 11 Squadrons fly a mixture of Mks 6s and the older, shorter-range Mk 3s. At the time of writing, each had nine 6s, three 3s, and a two-seater, although this could change in favour of Mk 6s. The squadrons' role is fourfold, to protect the integrity of UK airspace, to defend the UK in time of emergency, the defence of the fleet, and overseas deployment. This latter role has diminished, but the squadrons still have exchange visits with the French Air Force, and NATO squadrons, and visit their old base in Cyprus. The major continuing task is training, and this can take many forms, including combat air patrol (CAP).

The incoming 'enemy' against which the squadrons defend the coast of Britain in such exercises are likely to be RAF Jaguars, Buccaneers, or Harriers, coming in low and fast — often not more than a few feet above the sea. The attackers' brief will be to break through to the region of Flamborough Head. That of the Lightnings — on a check ride, a squadron would be likely to send up a Mk 3, and its 'T-bird' two-seater — to prevent them from breaking through, flying a CAP pattern up and down the coast, some 25 miles offshore.

Being such a 'gas-guzzler', each Lightning is always fully fuelled before departure with 1,200gal. At tactical speeds, each aircraft will burn 20gal/min, although in the sort of climb for which the aircraft is noted, with full afterburner selected, the rate will escalate to as much as 200gal/min. Pre-flight briefing for the pilot goes into great detail, covering the whole operation, from start-up, taxi-out (not less than 200yd between the aircraft, to prevent foreign object damage), take-off (rotation at 190mph), transit to the CAP area (not below 2,000ft, to avoid annoying the local population), tactics during the CAP operation, and return to base, with instructions about possible diversions.

In transit, the Lightnings will fly in pairs to protect the tail of the other. Arriving on station, they will loiter offshore, partnering each other about one mile apart, the crossover at the top and bottom of the patrol area being so engineered that one pilot always has his eyes to the east, from where the threat is expected to come.

Much of the advice against the arrival of the 'enemy' is simple fighter-pilot logic which would be equally understood by those who flew Camels and Spads in World War 1, and Spitfires and Hurricanes in World War 2 — use the sun and the clouds, assume that the aircraft which you are following has a friend who is about to follow you, watch your tail, watch your tail, watch your tail.

Not so comprehensible to the Spad or Camel pilot would be the advice to avoid using radar because it gives away the presence of the Lightning through the enemy's tail-warning device (although at certain points in combat it can be switched on to make the enemy break to order), and try not to pull more than 6G.

Will the incoming aircraft, whose brief is to represent as closely as possible the tactics of Soviet bombers and fighter-bombers, turn to fight when attacked, or will they press on towards the target? Coming round in a high G turn on the tail of an intruder means covering a wide arc of ground, and even with the high-dash speed of the Lightning a long chase to overhaul him, by which time he could be on his target. And so, Lightning pilots are taught to utilise to the full the extraordinary performance of their aircraft — climbing fast, and then descending on the adversary, rather than making wide turns. As one pilot at Binbrook commented, 'If we use the vertical, and the enemy decides to turn and engage, at that point, he is dead.'

What comes through very strongly at RAF Binbrook is the immense enthusiasm, even affection, which the men who continue to fly have for the Lightning. One senior officer there summed the aircraft up, and in doing so provided a fitting epilogue for this book on one of the great classic fighters, 'It is still one of the most-exhilerating of the high-performance aircraft that are around today. Even though it has a high workload, it is a fine pilot's aeroplane, and everyone enjoys flying it. We may not be as sophisticated as Jaguars and Phantoms, but although some people who are sent here are a little disappointed that they are not going to fly more-elegant types, they soon learn to like the Lightning, and they gain an immense amount of satisfaction from it.'

Above right:
Two No 11 Squadron Mk 6s hooked up to a Victor K1 tanker. Picture was taken during 1967. *MoD via P. Collins*

Right:
Mk 6 XS902 taking gas on board from Victor tanker XA937. Another picture, from an escorting two-seat Lightning, taken by Harry Kerr. *The Times*

Left:
Harry Kerr, a staff photographer of *The Times*, took this fine picture through the bomb aimer's window of a Canberra of a Lightning refuelling from a Victor tanker. *The Times*

Below:
Rare photograph of a Valiant tanker refuelling XM968, one of the early Mk 4 two-seaters, during development trials out of Warton, and before Valiants were withdrawn from service due to structural weaknesses. *BAe*

Right:
Picture taken at 30,000ft above northern Germany shows Mk 2A of No 19 Squadron about to take fuel from a Victor. MoD issued the print in November 1973, announcing that the upper parts of the aircraft are painted in a new, matt-green, low-visibility camouflage paint which was, at that time, being adopted throughout RAF Germany. *MoD*

Centre right:
Contrasting paint jobs; No 5 Squadron Lightning in the foreground has a new, two-tone grey paint job, while the same squadron's aircraft in the rear has the more traditional camouflage. Pitot tube of third Lightning, in the near foreground, is shrouded in a ground cover. *Author*

Bottom right:
Representative of the third group at Binbrook is this aircraft of the LTF, the Lightning Training Flight. XR726 was one of the earliest Mk 6s produced. *Author*

Above:
No 11 Squadron's two-seat T-bird gets a close inspection from groundcrew on the Binbrook flight line. Each of the two squadrons on the station has a T5 to complement its nine Mk 6s and three Mk 3s, but the Ts play the same warlike role as the single-seaters, as the Red Top missile shows. *Author*

Left:
Impressive line-up of Lightnings from the two Binbrook squadrons, and the LTF. Lightning pitot is long to keep it ahead of the shock wave at supersonic speeds. *Author*

Below:
Visiting Jaguar inserted into the Binbrook flight line looks small up against the bulky Lightnings which flank it. Aircraft in the foreground is a Lightning Training Flight Mk 5 XS456, wearing the old camouflage and tail badge; that to the rear is from No 5 Squadron, in the new grey paint. *Author*

Above:
As part of the scheme to make Lightnings less visible, the tail badges have been severely scaled down. XR726 Mk 6 has new grey paint and a little lion, while T5 XS417 two-seat still sports a large beast on its grey and green fin. *Author*

Below:
Refuelling in progress at Binbrook. Aircraft are mainly from No 11 Squadron, although two No 5 Squadron tails can be seen in the background. *Author*

Above right and right:
Repacking the aircraft's arrestor parachute is never the most-popular job on any Lightning squadron. Parachute emerges from below the lower jet pipe, but the wires which connect it with the aircraft are wound in a channel around the outside of both nozzles. Putting them back can be an intractable and finger-numbing task on a cold day. *Author*

Below:
No 5 Squadron Mk 6s on the apron at Binbrook. In the background, a visiting Tornado. *Author*

Left:
Replenishing the pilot's oxygen
supply on the Lightning is a
specialised job for the groundcrew,
requiring the use of protective
clothing. *Author*

Below:
Ventral gun pack has been removed
for servicing in the Binbrook hangars.
In the background stands a No 11
Squadron aircraft fitted with Red
Top. *Author*

Above:
Reputedly the highest-pressure aircraft tyre used by the RAF, at 325lb/sq in, the Lightning 'boot' is also reputed to cost around £300 a copy. *Author*

Above right:
With the familiar bullet fairing removed, the Lightning's radar is exposed for servicing. *Author*

Below:
Corner of one of the hangars at Binbrook contains aircraft from both squadrons, plus two aircraft stored under wraps. No 11 Squadron aircraft, nearest the camera, with its engines removed, is a Mk 3, XP695. The No 5 Squadron aircraft is a Mk 6, XS919. *Author*

Below:
Assorted Lightning hardware in a Binbrook hangar. Aircraft in store are rotated through the squadrons, and British Aerospace collaborates closely on airframe fatigue-alleviation programmes. *Author*

Bottom:
Gap in the top of the fuselage of this No 11 Squadron aircraft shows where the groundcrew have removed an engine. Spare Avon lies in the foreground of the picture. *Author*

Above:
Jacked-up for attention at Binbrook, this Mk 6 has had the forward part of its ventral bulge, containing the twin Aden 30mm cannon pack, removed. *Author*

Below:
Missiles ready to be strapped on to Lightnings lie in their carrying cradles in a Binbrook hangar. On the left, Firestreak, on the right, Red Top, all with their protective caps in place. *Author*

APPENDICES

1

LIGHTNING PRODUCTION

Prototypes: *P1* WG760 *P1A* WG763 (Sapphire engines; research aeroplanes) *P1B* XA847 (first British aircraft to fly at Mach 2 on 25 November 1958; now in RAF museum), XA853, XA856 (Avon RA24 engines; intake bullet). **Total: 5**

Pre-Production: XG307-XG313, XG325-XG333 (all Warton), XG334-XG336 (RAF Coltishall), XG337 (Warton). **Total: 20**

F Mark 1: XM134 (Warton), XM135-XM138 (RAF Coltishall with the Air Fighting Development Squadron which later became the Central Fighter Establishment) XM139-XM147, XM163-XM167 (RAF Coltishall with No 74 Squadron. A fatigue specimen, un-numbered, was also built). **Total: 19**

F Mark 1A: XM169 (Warton), XM170 (set aside for ground training), XM171-XM192, XM213-XM216 (RAF Wattisham with Nos 56 and 111 Squadrons. **Total: 28**

F Mark 2 and 2A: XN723 (A&AEE Boscombe Down; went to Rolls-Royce, Hucknall for engine development), XN724 (A&AEE Boscombe Down; went to Handling Squadron), XN725 (Warton), XN726 (RAF Binbrook), XN727-XN733 (RAF Leconfield), XN734 (Warton), XN735 XN767-XN770 (RAF Leconfield), XN771-XN773 (RAF Binbrook), XN774-XN776 (RAF Leconfield), XN777 (RAF Binbrook), XN778-XN797 (RAF Leconfield). XN795 was the 'prototype' Mk 2A although it differed from the 2A standard finally adopted. It was subsequently an MoD Tornado flight trials 'chase' aircraft at Warton
Of the Mk 2 and 2A, 15 went to Nos 19 and 92 Squadrons each and the rest to No 3 MU Lyneham, of which five subsequently went to the Royal Saudi Air Force as advance ('Magic Carpet') deliveries prior to delivery of production Mk 53s and 55s. The five were XN729, XN767, XN770, XN796 and XN797. the 31 Mk 2 aircraft following were converted to Mk 2A standard at Warton by a fly-in return-to-works programme from Nos 19 and 92 Squadrons in Germany from 1966 to 1970: XN726-XN728, XN730-XN733, XN735, XN771-XN778, XN780-XN784, XN786-XN793, XN795. XN725 and XN734 were fitted with Avon R146 engines and a fuel system and equipment as Mk 3

aeroplanes for development flying as 'prototypes'. XN734 was eventually purchased by BAC and used for Saudi project ground training at Warton. **Total: 44** (five converted to Mk 52)

F Mark 3: XP693-XP708, XP735-XP765, XR711-XR721, XR722 ('prototype' Mk 53 for Saudi Arabia), XR748-XR751 (delivered to Nos 74, 56, 111 and 23 Squadrons). **Total: 61** (one converted to Mk 53)

T Mark 4: XL628 (prototype Mk 4; company designation P11), XL629 (eventually went to Empire Test Pilots' School), XM966 (first production trainer; converted to second Mk 5 prototype), XM968-XM972 (RAF Middleton St George), XM973, XM974 (RAF Coltishall), XM987 (RAF Middleton St George), XM988 (RAF Leconfield), XM989 (RAF Wattisham), XM990 (RAF Middleton St George), XM992 (RAF Wattisham), XM993 (RAF Middleton St George), XM994, XM995 (RAF Leconfield), XM996, XM997 (RAF Middleton St George), XM989 and XM992 went to Royal Saudi Air Force as Mk 52 'Magic Carpet' deliveries. **Total: 21**

T Mark 5: XM967 (prototype Mk 5), XS416-XS423, XS449-XS459, XV328, XV329. **Total: 22**

F Mark 6 (Delivered to Nos 5, 74, 111 and 56 Squadrons): XR723-XR728, XR747, XR752 (first Mk 6 (interim standard) delivered with XR753 to the Air Fighting Development Squadron), XR753, XR754 (first Mk 6 (interim standard) to No 5 Squadron, RAF Binbrook), XR755-XR768 (first 'production' Mk 6 to fly), XR769-XR773, XS893-XS904, XS918-XS932, XS933 (on loan to Saudi Training School, Warton), XS934-XS938. **Total: 62**

F Mk 53: Royal Saudi Air Force 53-666-53-693, 53-695-53-700 (first flight 1 November 1966) Kuwait Air Force 53-412-53-423 (first flight June 1968). **Total: 46**

F Mk 55: 55-711-55-716 (first flight 3 November 1966)
Kuwait Air Force 55-410-55-411 (first flight 24 May 1968). **Total: 8**

Total Lightning Build: 337

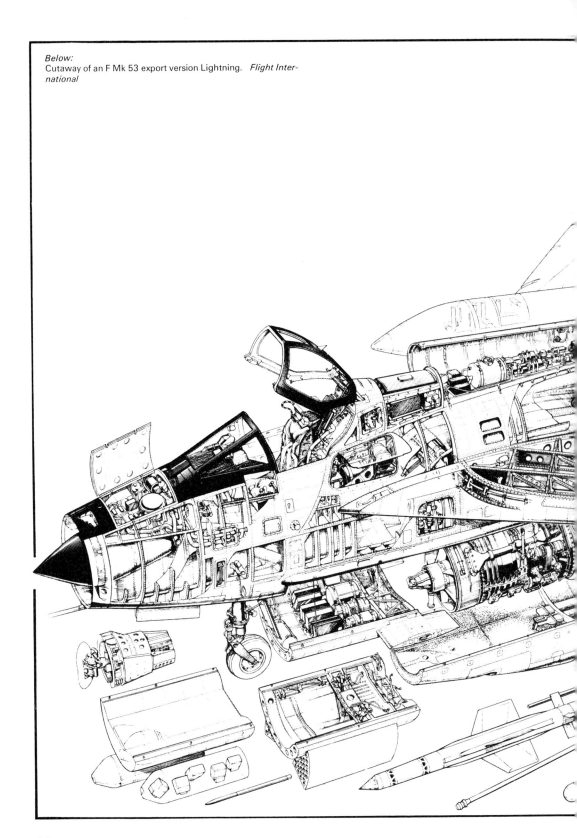

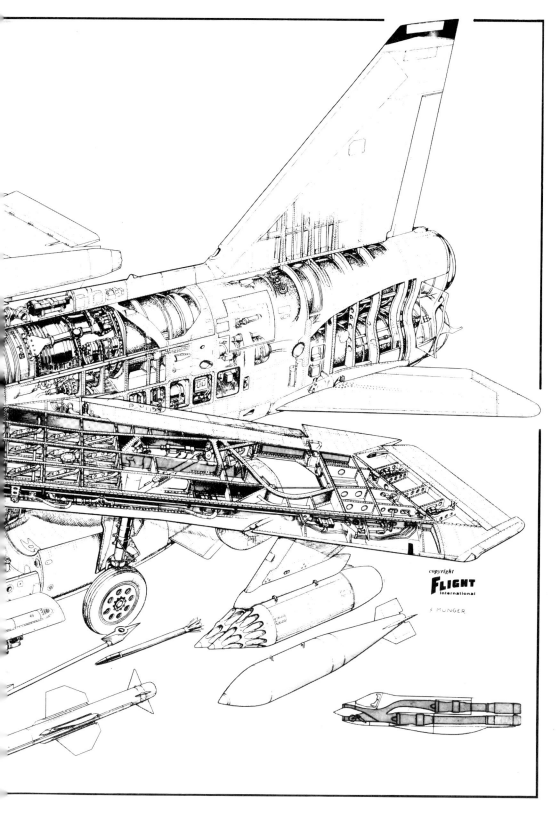

copyright

FLIGHT
international

S MUNGER

95

2
TECHNICAL SPECIFICATION

Data: Export variants

Span: 34.83ft (10.62m)

Length: 55.25ft (17.65m)

Height: 19.58ft (5.97m)

Armament: *Interceptor Role*

Two Red Top *or* Two Firestreak missiles

44×2in rockets

Two 30mm Aden cannon with 130 rounds each

Ground-Attack Role

36×68mm SNEB rockets in two Matra Type 155 launchers

Two 1,000lb (454kg) HE bombs

Two 30mm Aden cannon with 130 rounds each

Reconnaissance Role

Five Vinten Type 360 70mm cameras

1×6in f2.8 lens

2×3in f2.0 lens

2×1.75in f2.8 lens or 2×12in f2.0 lens

Weight: *Mk 53*

41,700lb (19,900kg) Max take-off with full combat load

Mk 55

39,530lb (17,947kg) with 2×Firestreak missiles

39,730lb (18,037kg) with 2×Red Top missiles

39,940lb (18,133kg) with 2×Firestreak and 2×30mm Aden cannon

40,140lb (18,224kg) with 2×Red Top and 2×30mm Aden cannon

Engines: Two Rolls-Royce Avon Mk 302-C

Max static thrust cold 11,100lb (5,039kg)

Max static thrust with max reheat 16,300lb (7,400kg)

Fuel capacity: 5,728lb (2,597kg) wings

4,872lb (2,209kg) ventral pack

4,320lb (1,960kg) (2×2, 160lb (980kg each) overwing tanks

14,920lb (6,766kg) total

Load Classification No: 35 (for rigid paved runways) 45 (for flexible paved runways)

Tyre Pressure: 350psi (24.6kg/sq cm) main wheels 240psi (16.8kg/sq cm) nose wheel

Ejector Seat: *Mk 53*

Martin-Baker Type BS4C Mk 2 for use from 90kts at zero altitude to 600kts IAS

Mk 55: Martin-Baker Type BS4B Mk 2 usable 90kts-600kts

Oxygen: Liquid Oxygen System (LOX) 3.5 litres capacity

Fire Warning and Extinguishing System: Graviner, automatic zone warning system; pilot initiated selective extinguishing

Radar and Fire Control System: Ferranti Radar Type AI23S including: Approach and attack computers; Search and attack display unit (cathode ray tube); Radar control and mode selector switch; Visual display cine recorder; Light fighter sight

Flight Control System: Integrated flight instrument display Type OR946 Phase 2; Air data system Mk 2; Navigation display unit; Master reference gyro; ILS (Instrument Landing System)

Standby Instruments: Artificial horizon Type 6H; Directional gyro indicator Type B; Compass Type E2B; Altimeter Mk 26; Air speed indicator Mk 18

Navigational Aids: Compass: Remote magnetic flux detector updates master gyro TACAN — with offset computer; UHF Homing; IFF Mk 10 with SIF

Radio: 1,750 channel combined UHF/VHF transmitter/receiver

UHF 'standby' set with two communications channels

Telebriefing ground communication facilities

Fuel: Avtur 50 or Avtag

Fuel Pumps: Two Type GBB131 1,600psi max (supply)

Two Type FBP104/111 60psi max (booster)

Two Type TPE101 14psi max (transfer)

Hydraulic System: Fluid OM-15 Integral pumps

Two Type 180 Mk 50/65 (services)

Two Type 220 Mk 37 (controls)

Pressure: 3,000psi (system), 1,500psi (brakes)

Electric Services:

Compressed air turbine driven alternator 200V 3-phase 400 c/s AC

Compress air turbine driven generator 28.5V DC

Back-up emergency supply battery 24V DC